OCR

AS/A LEVEL

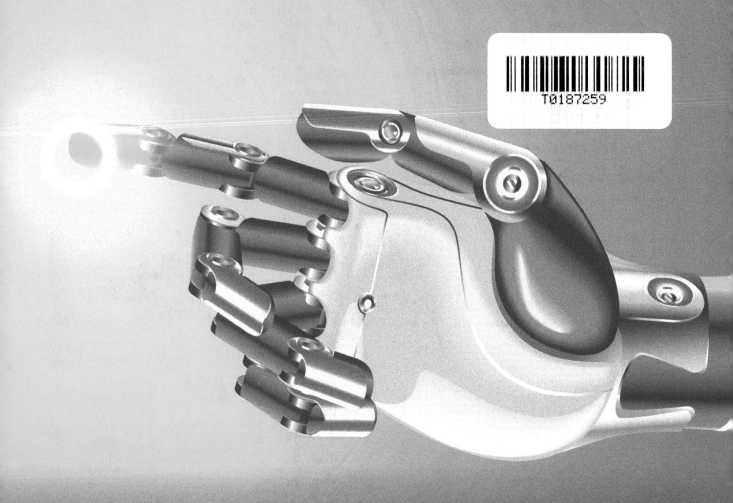

WORKBOOK

Computer Science 1

Computer systems

Sarah Lawrey

HODDER
EDUCATION
LEARN MORE

Contents

Computer systems

The central processing unit (CPU) 3

Types of processor 4

Input, output, storage and memory 5

Software and software development

Software 9

Applications generation 12

Software development 14

Types of programming language 16

Exchanging data

Compression 23

Encryption 24

Hashing 24

Databases 25

Networks 28

The internet 31

Data types, data structures and Boolean algebra

Data types 36

Data structures 40

Boolean algebra 42

Computer law and ethical, moral and social issues

Computer law 46

Ethical, moral and social issues 46

WORKBOOK

(1) This workbook will help you to prepare for the **Computer Science Computer Systems** exam.

(2) Your **exam** will include a range of questions requiring short and long responses. You will also have extended response questions.

(3) For **each topic** of the exam there are:
- stimulus materials including key terms and concepts
- short-answer questions that build up to exam-style questions
- space for you to write or plan your answers.

(4) **Answering the questions** will help you to build your skills and meet the assessment objectives AO1 (Demonstrate knowledge and understanding), AO2 (Apply knowledge and understanding), AO3 (Design, program and evaluate computer systems).

(5) You still need to read your textbook and refer to your revision guides and lesson notes.

(6) Content specific to A level only is indicated by a red line in the margin.

(7) Marks available are indicated for all questions so that you can gauge the level of detail required in your answers.

(8) Timings are given for the exam-style questions to make your practice as realistic as possible.

(9) Answers are available at:
www.hoddereducation.co.uk/workbookanswers

Computer systems

The central processing unit (CPU)

The central processing unit (CPU) is a fundamental part of a computer system. It is responsible for fetching every instruction given to the computer, decoding it and executing it. It is a very active component that is capable of processing billions of instructions per second.

The CPU has a number of different components that it uses to process instructions. A single cycle of processing an instruction is called the fetch–decode–execute cycle. Three main factors can affect the performance of a CPU: clock speed, number of cores and cache size.

A CPU will have a particular structure, such as the von Neumann or Harvard architecture. The CPU is small in size but has a very big role to play.

1 **State the main role of the CPU.** [1 mark]

....

....

2 **Identify three registers that are used in the CPU.** [3 marks]

....

....

....

3 **Identify three buses that are used in the CPU.** [3 marks]

....

....

....

4 **Describe the role of the cache in the CPU.** [3 marks]

....

....

....

....

....

5 **Explain the difference between the von Neumann and the Harvard architecture.** [4 marks]

....

....

....

....

Pipelining

Most CPUs make use of pipelining. This allows the CPU to process an instruction whilst fetching the next instruction.

6 **Describe how a processor would operate if it cannot make use of pipelining.** *2 marks*

....

....

....

....

Types of processor

There are different types of processor: two of these are CISC and RISC.

CISC processors often contain a large set of instructions for both simple and complex procedures. CISC processors have separate instructions for each task that the processor could be required to do.

RISC processors use a highly optimised set of instructions that are designed to require fewer cycles per execution of the instruction. RISC processors often contain a smaller set of instructions comprised of those that are the most frequently used. Unlike CISC processors, RISC processors normally have several tasks condensed into a single instruction.

The speed of the processor can be increased using parallel processing. This is when a processor can carry out multiple tasks simultaneously. Two types of parallel processing are SIMD and MIMD. In SIMD processing, the same operation is performed on multiple data simultaneously. This is useful for improving the performance of the processor with multimedia. In MIMD processing, different instructions are performed on different data simultaneously. A processor needs to be multicore to allow MIMD processing.

7 **State what is meant by parallel processing.** *1 mark*

....

....

8 **Give one benefit of parallel processing.** *1 mark*

....

....

9 **Explain one difference between a CISC and a RISC processor.** *2 marks*

....

....

....

....

10 **Explain one difference between SIMD and MIMD processing.** *2 marks*

....

....

....

....

Graphics processing unit (GPU)

GPUs are designed to process calculations for graphics. They have an instruction set specifically designed for this. GPUs will often use SIMD processing. The capabilities of GPUs are sometimes used for more than processing graphics. GPUs are now used for tasks such as crypto-currency mining, cracking passwords and machine learning.

11 **Explain why a GPU could be used to crack passwords.**

....

....

....

....

Input, output, storage and memory

Many computer systems have input, output and storage. Computer systems often have RAM and ROM storage. RAM is volatile; this means the contents are lost when power is disconnected. ROM is non-volatile; this means the contents are retained when power is disconnected. RAM is used to store the programs and data that are currently in use, while ROM is used to store the boot-up instructions.

There are three main type of storage: magnetic, flash and optical. Magnetic storage devices use magnets to record data on rotating magnetic plates. An example is a hard disk drive. Flash storage devices use positive and negative charges to record data onto cells that are made up of transistors. Unlike magnetic storage devices, flash storage devices do not have any moving parts. An example is a solid-state drive. Optical storage uses a beam of light and a lens to record data onto a disk. Data is stored in pits and lands on the surface of the disk. An example is a CD.

Another way of storing data is using virtual storage. Virtual storage is when data is stored in a cloud-based system and accessed using an internet connection. The alternative would be storing data locally on the computer. Virtual storage is only virtual in name; it is still physical storage and is normally owned and managed by a third party.

12 **State two characteristics of RAM.**

....

....

....

....

....

....

13 **State two characteristics of ROM.**

....

....

....

....

....

....

14 Give two benefits of virtual storage. 2 marks

....

....

....

....

15 Explain the difference between magnetic storage and flash storage. 4 marks

....

....

....

....

....

....

....

16 Describe how data is stored by an optical storage device. 4 marks

....

....

....

....

....

....

Exam-style questions

35

17 Tina has a computer system that has a dual core, 2 GHz processor. She wants to upgrade her processor as she has a new job that requires her to use her computer for high-quality video editing.

Explain the upgrades she can make to the processor and what effect it will have on the performance. 4 marks

....

....

....

....

....

....

18 Describe how an instruction and data is fetched by the CPU, including the registers and buses used. **5 marks**

....

....

....

....

....

....

....

....

....

....

19 Explain why a RISC processor would be faster than a CISC processor. **4 marks**

....

....

....

....

....

....

....

....

....

....

20 Explain why a processor would need to be multicore for MIMD processing. **3 marks**

....

....

....

....

....

....

....

21 Explain why flash storage is preferred to magnetic storage in mobile devices. 4 marks

....

....

....

....

....

....

....

22 Explain why a personal computer system needs both RAM and ROM. 6 marks

....

....

....

....

....

....

....

....

....

....

....

....

Software and software development

Software

The operating system is software that gets loaded by the computer after it has booted up. The boot-up routine is normally carried out by the BIOS. The BIOS will usually carry out the POST test and once this is complete it will boot the computer. The operating system is then loaded into memory.

The operating system is software that is designed to control and manage the hardware in and connected to the computer, and all other software. It is responsible for tasks such as file management, memory management, peripheral management, software installation, security and providing an interface for the user. Without an operating system, it would be very difficult, if not impossible, to use a computer system. Operating systems are usually required to communicate with several different devices. These devices are often manufactured by different companies. This can cause communication issues. To allow communication to occur between the different devices and the computer system, software called drivers are used.

1. **Memory management is one task performed by an operating system. Identify four other tasks performed by an operating system.**

....

....

....

....

2. **Identify the software used by the operating system to allow communication with many different devices.**

....

3. **Explain why it would not be possible to use a computer without an operating system.**

....

....

....

....

4. **Explain the role and position of the kernel in an operating system.**

....

....

....

....

....

Different types of operating system

There are a several different types of operating system. These include distributed, embedded, multi-tasking, multi-user and real time.

A distributed operating system involves a group of computers working together on a single task. Each computer is responsible for part of the task. A distributed operating system is used to co-ordinate the computers to enable them to complete the task. An embedded computer, such as a washing machine, may have an embedded operating system. This kind of operating system is more specifically tailored for the embedded computer, to increase efficiency.

A multi-tasking operating system is one that can run several programs simultaneously. This is the most common type of operating system found on the computers we use in our daily lives. It allows us to do tasks such as listen to music whilst typing into a document, occasionally checking our social media.

A multi-user operating system is one that allows multiple users to be using the computer's resources simultaneously. This type of operating system often exists on a mainframe computer, where many users may be accessing the data at a given time.

A real-time operating system is one that has a rapid response time. It completes the action requested within a fraction of a second.

It is possible for a computer to have more than one type of operating system. For example, the computers we use on a daily basis will most likely be both multi-tasking and real time.

5 **A washing machine uses an embedded operating system. Identify three other devices that would use an embedded operating system.** *3 marks*

....

....

....

....

6 **Identify the type of operating system that air traffic control would need to use.** *1 mark*

....

....

7 **Give two benefits of a distributed operating system.** *2 marks*

....

....

....

....

Memory management

One responsibility of the operating system is memory management. This includes how the memory resources available in the computer are shared. One type of memory management that a computer can use is paging. Paging is when a computer retrieves data stored in secondary storage and brings it into RAM. In paging, the memory is divided into physical units of the same size. Each of these units is known as a page. Another type of memory management is segmentation. In segmentation, the memory is divided into logical units of varying size. Each of these units is known as a segment. Each segment will normally be a logical grouping of code, such as a procedure.

Explain what would happen if memory management wasn't carried out by the operating system.

....

....

....

....

....

....

Explain what paging and segmentation are and how an operating system would make use of both of them .

....

....

....

....

....

....

....

....

....

....

....

....

Interrupts

An interrupt does exactly what is sounds like it should, it interrupts! This service is needed because a computer needs to know when to give its attention to a different task. A device sends a signal to the CPU; this signal is known as an interrupt. Each interrupt has a level of urgency and the operating system manages which interrupt signals will be dealt with first. The operating system has a function called an interrupt service routine that carries out this responsibility.

Scheduling

An operating system that is multi-tasking needs to make sure that tasks are run simultaneously. It is important to understand that they aren't actually run simultaneously; the computer switches between them during fractions of seconds to make them appear to be run simultaneously. For this to occur an operating system needs to have a scheduler. A scheduler manages the time allocated to the different tasks a CPU is currently processing. It can use several different algorithms to do this, these include round robin, first come first served, multi-level feedback queues, shortest job first and shortest remaining time.

Virtual machines

A virtual machine is effectively creating a computer within a computer. It is a piece of software that is run on a computer, but is designed to behave like a different computer. A common application of this is to have multiple operating systems on a single computer. Each operating system will be a virtual machine.

10　Describe the role of a scheduler in an operating system.　

....

....

....

....

....

11　Will is creating an Android game and needs to test it in an Android environment.
He doesn't have an Android device available to test it on. Explain how Will could test
the device using his computer.　

....

....

....

....

....

Applications generation

Applications are the programs that we use daily to complete our everyday tasks. Some examples of application software are a word processor, a spreadsheet package, a web browser and utility software.

Utility software normally has a small, dedicated purpose, for example defragmenting the hard drive, scanning for viruses, compressing files or creating backups. Utility software is designed to maintain a computer system.

Applications can be open source or closed source. When software is open source, the source code for it is freely accessible to anyone. This means that users can modify the code to change the functionality of the software. When software is closed source, the source code is not accessible to anyone but the creator. There are benefits and drawbacks of both open source and closed source software. One benefit of open source software is that it is mostly free (without cost). One drawback of open source software is that it may not have been tested properly if the resources are not available to do this. One benefit of closed source software is that it has been thoroughly tested before release. However, one drawback of closed source software is that it can be expensive.

12　Defragmentation is one example of utility software. Give four other examples of
utility software.　

....

....

....

....

....

....

13 **Describe the operation of defragmentation.**

14 **Give two benefits of open source software.**

15 **Give two drawbacks of closed source software.**

Assemblers, compilers and interpreters

When a programmer creates an application, a translator is needed to convert the program to machine code. This is because processors only understand machine code. Depending on the language the programmer has used, an interpreter, a compiler or an assembler will be used.

If the programmer has written the program in assembly code, an assembler will be used. If the programmer has written the program in a high-level language, an interpreter or a compiler will be used.

An interpreter converts and runs each line of code at a time. If it hits an error, it will stop running the code and notify the user there is an error in the program.

A compiler converts the whole program at once before running it. It will not run if an error is found and will produce an error report. An executable file is created by the compiler.

A compiler operates by going through several stages of compilation. These are lexical analysis, syntax analysis, code generation and optimisation.

Libraries

When writing a program, a programmer may use libraries. A library is a pre-programmed routine that can be used to perform a specific task in the program. If libraries have been used in a program, a linker or a loader will be required after the code has been optimised. A static linker brings all the code for the library into the program as it is compiled. A dynamic linker loads and links the libraries at run time. A loader is also used that is responsible for loading the program into memory. It is often thought that a dynamic linker is a type of loader also.

Software development

Building software can be challenging, time consuming and expensive. It often requires a certain approach depending on the amount of time and funds available. There are several different models that can be followed when building software: the waterfall model, agile programming, extreme programming, the spiral model and rapid application development.

Methodologies

The waterfall model is a well-known, but rather outdated model. It consists of several stages of development that are completed one after the other. These include analysis, design, development, testing, implementation and maintenance. Agile methodologies are when software is produced through an iterative process. An example of an agile methodology is extreme programming. This relies on very short development cycles. The spiral model is more risk-driven. It is also an iterative process that passes through four main stages repeatedly: determining objectives, identifying and resolving risks, development and testing, and planning the next iteration.

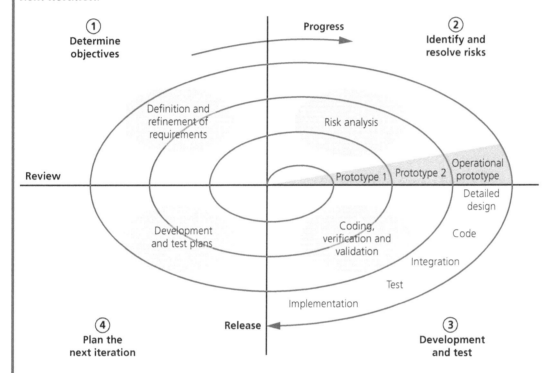

Rapid application development revolves around the use of prototypes. A prototype is produced, feedback is sought and this then informs the development of the next prototype.

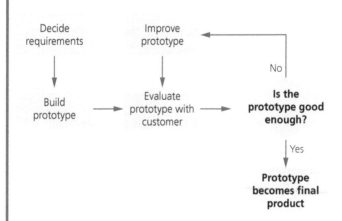

Each software development model has benefits and drawbacks. The waterfall model is simple and easy to manage but requires a lot of time. Agile methodologies can produce software in a much shorter time than the waterfall model. The spiral model is very good for larger projects that may have a greater level of risk. Rapid application works effectively for projects that don't have clear requirements as it allows them to evolve as the prototypes are built.

16 Draw a diagram to represent the waterfall model.

17 Give two benefits of the waterfall model.

....

....

....

....

18 Give one benefit and one drawback of the spiral model.

....

....

....

....

19 Explain what is meant by pair programming and identify which software development method uses it.

....

....

....

....

....

....

....

20 A company needs to create a new data management system in a short time scale. They don't know what all the requirements of the system will be yet, as their business service is evolving. State which software development cycle would be most suitable for the company to use. Justify your choice. 6 marks

....

....

....

....

....

....

....

....

....

Types of programming language

Programmers can use several different programming paradigms to create computer programs. Each programming paradigm has a different approach to how to create the program.

One programming paradigm is procedural programming. This programming paradigm is based around the creation of subroutines that can be called at any point in the program.

21 Define what is meant by a programming paradigm. 1 mark

....

22 Explain what is meant by the procedural programming paradigm. 4 marks

....

....

....

....

....

....

There are several alternative programming paradigms. These include declarative, imperative, functional and object-oriented. Declarative programming is about telling the program what it should be achieving, whereas imperative programming should tell the program how to achieve it. Functional programming is a declarative approach that is focused around building a collection of functions. Object-oriented programming focuses on the development of objects rather than actions. It focuses on incorporating both data and processes, rather than treating them as separate elements.

Object-oriented programming

Object-oriented programming involves the use of classes, objects, methods, attributes, inheritance, encapsulation and polymorphism.

A class is like a template. In a class we define the attributes and methods that we want the class to have. The attributes are the data and the methods are the processes that we need for the class. To initialise each attribute in an object, a constructor is used.

Encapsulation is a fundamental aspect of object-oriented programming. The act of incorporating the data and processes together in a class is an example of encapsulation. The use of get and set methods to access, amend and return data is also an example of encapsulation.

Inheritance is a fundamental aspect of object-oriented programming. Often, a system will require multiple classes. This could involve a parent class that contains the information that is applicable to all objects, then child classes are created that contain more specific information. On most occasions, a child class will inherit the attributes and methods from the parent class. This means that if an object is created based on a child class, it will carry out all the requirements of that class and of those in the parent class.

Polymorphism is also a fundamental aspect of object-oriented programming. This refers to the ability to create objects differently depending on their data type or class. There are many examples in object-oriented programming that fall into the definition of polymorphism. One example would be a method that is defined in a parent class but overridden in a child class, dependent on certain circumstances.

23 **State what is meant by a class.**

....

....

....

24 **State what is meant by an object.**

....

....

....

25 **Explain what is meant by encapsulation.**

....

....

....

26 **State three things that are defined in a class diagram.**

....

....

....

....

....

27 Create a class diagram to show what a class could look like for a bank account.

3 marks

28 The class 'bank account' is now a parent class. It has two child classes of 'current account' and 'savings account'. Expand and adapt your class diagram to include the child classes.

10 marks

29 The parent class has a method to calculate interest. This method is overwritten in the child class for the savings account if the customer has a variable rate of interest applied. State what this is an example of.

1 mark

Assembly language (Little Man Computer)

One language that computer programs are written in is assembly language. All processors will convert any computer program to binary to be processed. Assembly language is a low-level computer language that can be converted very quickly.

A simulation called Little Man Computer can be used to see how the CPU processes assembly code. There are several versions of the simulation available via the internet. Each instruction in LMC has an opcode and an operand. The opcode is the mnemonic that defines that action that takes place, for example LDA, and the operand is the part that the action is performed on, for example, Num1.

Mnemonic	Instruction
ADD	Add
SUB	Subtract
STA	Store
LDA	Load
BRA	Branch always
BRZ	Branch if zero
BRP	Branch if zero or positive
INP	Input
OUT	Output
HLT	End program
DAT	Data location

Table 1 The opcodes that can be used in LMC

30 State where data is initially stored before it is fetched into the CPU.

31 Explain the function of the LDA command.

32 Write a program for LMC that will loop five times, outputting a value each time that is stored in a location named B. After it has looped five times, it outputs a value stored in a location named A and stops.

Memory addressing

When we need to access memory locations in assembly code we can use several different methods. These include direct, indirect, immediate and indexed addressing.

In direct addressing, the assembly code refers directly to a location in memory that we want to put the data. For example:

```
INP

STA 5     HLT
```

The instruction to store the input directly points to address location 5.

In indirect addressing, the assembly code refers indirectly to an address in memory of data that is required. Therefore, STA 5 would now mean that whatever value is stored in address 5 would be the address of the value that needs loading into the accumulator. For example, if 12 was stored in address 5, then the value stored in address 12 would be loaded into the accumulator.

In immediate addressing, the operand value is the actual value that we require in the accumulator. Therefore, STA 5 would now mean that we want 5 in the accumulator.

In indexed addressing, the index register is used. The value stored in the index register is the address required. The index register can be incremented to change the value for the address required.

Exam-style questions

(50)

33 Write an algorithm to explain how data is retrieved from virtual memory.   (6 marks)

34 Explain how an interrupt service routine operates.   (6 marks)

35 Luke has a program that he wants to send to his friend Alice. He wants Alice to just be able to run the code. He doesn't want to give her access to the source code. State which translator Luke should use. Justify your choice. `3 marks`

....

....

....

....

....

36 Nancy uses an interpreter to create code for her school project. Explain why Nancy would use an interpreter rather than a compiler while creating the code. `4 marks`

....

....

....

....

....

....

....

37 Nancy has finished creating the code and now wants to compile it. She has used libraries when creating her code. Explain how Nancy's code is compiled. `9 marks`

....

....

....

....

....

....

....

....

....

....

....

....

38 Many companies now prefer agile software development methods rather than the classic waterfall lifecycle. Discuss why this change has occurred. **9 marks**

39 Explain the difference between declarative and imperative programming. **5 marks**

40 Write an assembly code program for a guessing game. **8 marks**

The program must:
- allow the number to be guessed to be input
- allow the number being guessed to be input
- allow a user five tries to guess the number
- output the number 1 if the number is guessed correctly and terminate the program
- output the number 0 if after five tries the number is not guessed correctly and terminate the program

Write your answer on a separate sheet of paper.

Exchanging data

Compression

When data is exchanged between different systems we often need to compress it to make the process more efficient. There are two methods of compression that can be used, lossy and lossless.

In lossy compression, the size of the file is reduced by permanently removing some of the data. The data that is targeted for removal is data that is thought to be the least important detail. This will reduce the quality of the file, but possibly not in a way that most people would notice.

In lossless compression, the size of the file is reduced by temporarily changing the data it contains, but not removing any of it. The original data can be restored when the file is decompressed. Two methods of lossless compression are run-length encoding and dictionary encoding.

Run-length encoding is used when repeating values occur consecutively. These values can be compressed by recording the number of repetitions.

Dictionary encoding is when repeating values are encoded using a dictionary. Each character or word is given an index in the dictionary.

1. State what is meant by compression.

....

....

....

2. Identify the two types of compression that can be used.

....

....

....

3. Explain why lossy compression is not suitable for a text file.

....

....

....

....

4. Consider the phrase: 'Every day, in every way, I am getting better and better'.
   a. Encode the message using run-length encoding.

....

....

....

....

Encode the message using dictionary encoding.

Explain which encoding method is better and why.

....

....

....

....

....

....

....

....

Encryption

When data is exchanged between different systems we often need to encrypt it. This means that if the data is stolen, it will be meaningless to the perpetrator. Before data is encrypted it is known as plain text. Data that has been encrypted is known as cypher text. A key is used to encrypt data that is a form of encryption algorithm. There are different types of encryption that can be used: these include symmetric and asymmetric.

In symmetric encryption, a single key is used. The same key is used to both encrypt and decrypt the data.

In asymmetric encryption, two different keys are used. One key is known as a public key and the other a private key. The public key is used to encrypt the data. To decrypt the data, the public key must be applied with the private key.

Hashing

Hashing is like encryption, in that data is effectively encrypted, but data cannot be directly decrypted in hashing. It is basically a one-way process. An example of a use for hashing could be for the storage of passwords. A company may need to store users' passwords for their accounts. The company probably does not want to store the actual password string, because if it was hacked, it would be very easy for the hacker to steal all the passwords. Therefore, a hash function (also known a hash algorithm) could be applied to the password before it is stored. This would mean that all that is stored is the hash version of the password. When a user enters their password, the hash function is applied again to see if the outcome matches the version stored.

5 State what is meant by an encryption key.

....

....

6 State what is meant by a hash function.

....

....

7 Describe how an encryption key could be made more secure.

....

....

....

....

8 Explain the difference between encryption and hashing.

....

....

....

....

....

Databases

A database is a collection of data that is related. A flat-file database has a single table and a relational database has multiple tables with a relationship linking them together. A primary key is a unique field in a database and a foreign key is a primary key in one table that appears in another table to create a link. There are several methods that can be used to access data in a database. This includes serial and sequential access.

In serial access, each record will be looked at until the record required is found. If the record required is close to the top of the table, then access will be relatively quick, but if it is near the bottom of a large table, access will be slow.

In sequential access, a similar process to serial occurs in that each record is looked at; it is just that the records have been organised into a certain order to aid the process. Sequential access can make use of an index. For example, if customers are put into alphabetic order, an index of A, B, C etc. can be used. If a customer has a name beginning with D, each index can be looked at until D is found, then all D records can be looked at until the customer is found.

9 State what is meant by a flat-file database.

....

....

10 **Explain what a primary key is and why it is needed.** 2 marks

....

....

....

....

11 **State the role of a foreign key.** 1 mark

....

....

12 **Describe how Mrs Alice Jones would be found using serial access.** 2 marks

....

....

....

....

Normalisation

A process called normalisation can be used to separate the data, to avoid the issue of data redundancy. Data that is unnormalised (UNF/0NF) has repeated entries of data and it may also have data that is not atomic.

The first stage of normalisation is first normal form 1NF. For 1NF, the following rules are applied:

- The table will not have any repeating entries of data, or repeating fields.
- All the fields in the database will be atomic.
- Each record in the database will be unique and have a unique identifier.

The second stage of normalisation is second normal form 2NF. For 2NF, the following rules are applied:

- Data must be in 1NF.
- Any data that is not dependent on the primary key of a table will be separated into a different table.

The third stage of normalisation is third normal form 3NF. For 3NF, the following rules are applied:

- Data must be in 2NF.
- Any fields that are not directly related to each other are given further separation.

Once a database is normalised, relationships can be created between each table in the database, using the primary key and linking it to the foreign key in another table.

Data integrity is a very important issue in a database and measures that can be taken to maintain data integrity are imperative. One way of maintaining data integrity is referential integrity. This is where a process is applied to stop actions performed on a database creating inconsistent data. The process of normalisation naturally improves data integrity, because it uses referential integrity.

13 **State what is meant by normalising a database.** 1 mark

....

....

14 Consider the following database.

Artist/Band	Contact details	Booking date	Venue	Fee	Manager/Agent
PopRUs	poprus@us.com 07777777771	01/01/2019	The Arena, Play St, London, LN1 1LN	2000	Mandy's Music
Play That Guitar	playthatguitar@us.com 07777777772	02/01/2019	The Hall, Sing St, Manchester, M1 1MM	3500	Jenna Jackson
Jonesy Jones	jonesyjones@us.com 07777777773	02/01/2019	The Arena, Play St, London, LN1 1LN	3000	Jenna Jackson
The Sing Songers	singsongers@us.com 07777777774	03/01/2019	The Academy, Guitar St, Birmingham, B1 1BB	2500	Billy Bob
Up The Charts	upthecharts@us.com 07777777775	03/01/2019	The Hall, Sing St, Manchester, M1 1MM	2500	StarsRUs
ThrashOut	thrashout@us.com 07777777776	04/01/2019	The Arena, Play St, London, LN1 1LN	2000	Billy Bob
Jonesy Jones	jonesyjones@us.com 07777777773	05/01/2019	The Hall, Sing St, Manchester, M1 1MM	2500	Jenna Jackson
PopRUs	poprus@us.com 07777777771	05/01/2019	The Academy, Guitar St, Birmingham, B1 1BB	2500	Mandy's Music
Up The Charts	upthecharts@us.com 07777777775	06/01/2019	The Academy, Guitar St, Birmingham, B1 1BB	3000	StarsRUs

   a   **Normalise the database to 1NF.**

   b   **Normalise the database to 2NF.**

   c   **Normalise the database to 3NF.**

Write your answers on a separate sheet of paper.

Structured query language (SQL)

To search a database, a language called SQL can be used. There are several SQL commands that you need to be able to use.

SELECT	Used to say what data will be selected, often the name of a field.
FROM	Used to say where the data will be selected from, often the name of a table.
WHERE	Used for a condition that needs to be applied.
LIKE	Used to further refine a condition, for example a wildcard.
AND	An operator used with multiple conditions.
OR	An operator used with multiple conditions.
DELETE	Used to remove data.
INSERT	Used to add data.
DROP	Used to remove whole sections of data, for example a table.
JOIN	Used to combine data.

Table 2 SQL commands

These commands can be combined to create an SQL search.

An example of an SQL search would be:

```
SELECT "CustomerForename", "CustomerSurname" FROM "tblCustomers" WHERE
   "MailingList" = "Yes" AND "NewsLetterSent" = "No"
```

This search is designed to return the names of all customers who are signed up to the mailing list but haven't been sent a newsletter.

ACID rules

> When any additions or amends are made to a database, this is called a transaction. To protect the integrity of the data in a database, transactions should conform to certain rules. These rules should uphold the ACID properties: atomicity, consistency, isolation and durability.

Networks

Many organisations and individuals make use of a network. There are several different types of network, these include private networks, virtual networks, LANs and WANs. Networks can have many different models: two of these are client–server and peer-to-peer.

A client–server network has two main types of computer, a client and a server. The server is the centre of the network and provides services and data for the clients on the network.

A peer-to-peer network does not have a central system to manage the network. The management of the network is the responsibility of each individual peer.

Each network can also have a different structure, including bus, ring, star and mesh.

Protocols

For communication to be effective using a network, there are several protocols and standards that need to be upheld. Protocols are rules that govern how a network operates. They make it possible for many different devices to communicate using a network. Protocols are normally made up of layers. This is an inbuilt form of abstraction. Each layer in the protocol has a different responsibility. One protocol that is commonly used is the TCP/IP protocol. This is used in communication across the internet. The TCP/IP protocol has four layers.

Layer	Responsibility
Application layer	To collect and distribute data, making sure it suitable for transmission.
Transport layer	To establish and terminate connections between devices. To perform error detection and establish the speed data is sent.
Internet layer	To establish a route from the sender to the receiver.
Network/Link layer	To makes sure the transmission media is in place.

Table 3 TCP/IP layers

Some protocols and systems can have as many as seven layers, for example the OSI model.

Data can be exchanged across a network using packet switch or circuit switching. When we send data across a network, we divide it into packets. In circuit switching, packets are sent across a set route. In packet switching, packets are sent across any route that is available.

---

15 State what is meant by a network. `1 mark`

....

....

....

....

16 State what is meant by a protocol. `1 mark`

....

....

....

....

17 Draw a diagram to represent a star topology network structure.

18 Explain the difference between a client–server and a peer-to-peer network.

....

....

....

....

....

....

19 Draw a diagram to represent how data is sent in a circuit-switching network.

20 Draw a diagram to represent how data is sent in a packet-switching network.

4 marks

Network security

One of the issues with networks is that they are often subjected to many different threats. These include malware, brute-force attacks, denial-of-service attacks and theft of data. There are several ways a network can be protected, such as a firewall or a proxy server. Data being transmitted across the network can also be protected through encryption. This would make the data meaningless if it was stolen. Each method of protection cannot guarantee an attack will not occur, but it can make the possibility far more difficult.

Hardware

A network can contain several different components. These include a network interface card, a router, a switch, wireless access points, transmission media and possibly a domain name server.

21 State three types of transmission media that can be used in a network.

3 marks

22 Describe the role of a router in a network.

2 marks

Describe the role of a domain name server in the internet.

....

....

....

....

....

....

....

....

The internet

Web authoring tools

HTML is the most basic language used to author web pages. There are several HTML tags you need to be able to use. CSS is a formatting method that is used to create a consistent style for web pages. There are a number of CSS properties that you need to be able to use.

JavaScript is a programming language that is used to add interactivity to web pages. You need to be able to create inputs and outputs using JavaScript commands.

Complete the table to describe the use of each of the HTML tags listed.

Tag	Use
<html>	
<link>	
<title>	
<body>	
<h1><h2><h3>	
<img>	
<a>	
<div>	
<form>	
<input>	
<p>	
<li>	
<ol>	
<ul>	
<script>	

State what a '#' is used for in CSS.

....

....

26 State what a ';' is used for in CSS. *(1 mark)*

....

....

....

27 Write CSS code for the following template. *(5 marks)*

- All headings must be Arial, point size 22 and dark blue.
- Information boxes must have a background colour of pale blue and a black border that has a width of 5 pixels, and all text must be Arial, point size 16 and black.

....

....

....

....

....

....

....

....

....

....

....

....

....

....

....

Search engines

Search engines search the world wide web for web pages that match the keywords entered into the search bar. To do this they use a complex search algorithm. Search engines build up large indexes of web pages to make the searching process more efficient. Organisations add meta data to the header of their website. This meta data contains keywords that the search engine can easily find.

It is important that a search engine can quickly provide the user with a list of useful web pages that match their search criteria. One of the most successful tools in providing this service is the Pagerank algorithm. This algorithm looks at more than the content of the web page. It also assesses how many other web pages are linked to a web page and gives it a higher ranking based on this.

Client- and server-side processing

The processing of data that is exchanged over the internet can be carried out in two ways, at either the client side or the server side. When data is processed at the client side, it reduces the load on the server. However, when data is processed at the server side, data can be kept more secure.

28 **State what is meant by a search engine index.**

....

....

29 **Describe how the Pagerank algorithm works.**

....

....

....

....

....

....

....

....

Exam-style questions

30 **Describe how asymmetric encryption is used to send data securely.** 6 marks

....

....

....

....

....

....

....

....

....

....

....

....

....

The table is called Customer.

Cust no	Title	Forename	Surname	House no	Street	Town	Postcode	Order no
1001	Mr	Benny	Jones	1	New Street	New Town	NS1 1NT	001
1002	Mrs	Emily	Rose	1	Old Street	Old Town	OS1 1OS	002
1003	Miss	Victoria	Bloom	2	New Street	New Town	NS1 1NT	003
1004	Mr	Luke	Miles	2	Old Street	Old Town	OS1 1OS	004
1005	Mrs	Alice	Jones	3	New Street	New Town	NS1 1NT	005
1006	Mr	John	Smith	3	Old Street	Old Town	OS1 1OS	006

a   Write an SQL statement that would return the forename of all customers who live in Old Town.

b   Write an SQL statement that would return the full names and titles of all customers who live in New Town.

c   Write an SQL statement that would return the titles and surnames of all customers who live in Old Town and have an order number greater than 003.

32 Describe how a firewall can be used to improve the security of a network. `4 marks`

....

....

....

....

....

....

....

33 Give two benefits and one drawback of using a network. `3 marks`

....

....

....

....

....

34 Explain the role of the transport layer in the TCP/IP protocol. `4 marks`

....

....

....

....

....

....

....

35 State two reasons why a company would choose to have client-side processing. `4 marks`

....

....

....

....

....

Data types, data structures and Boolean algebra

Data types

Data can be of many different types. These include string, character, integer, real and Boolean. We need to assign a suitable data type to any data we store to make sure that we can use it in the most efficient way.

Representing positive integers

All data needs to be converted to binary in order to be processed by a computer system. It is important to know how to represent a positive integer as binary.

It is useful to be able to convert positive integers to hexadecimal. Hexadecimal is often used instead of binary as it is a shorter method of representation and can be easier to read. To convert a positive integer to hexadecimal, a simple method is to divide the number by 16, this will be the number of the unit 16 needed, and then the remainder is the number of 1s needed.

In hexadecimal notation, numbers 1 to 9 are the same, but 10 to 15 are represented by the characters A to F. Therefore, 178 in hexadecimal notation is B2. If 16 of the unit 16 need to be used, then the next unit is required, which is 256.

1. **Convert the denary value 101 to binary.** — *1 mark*

2. **Convert the denary value 326 to binary.** — *1 mark*

3. **Convert the binary value 11001111 to denary.** — *1 mark*

4. **Convert the binary value 1011001101 to denary.** — *1 mark*

5. **Convert the denary value 233 to hexadecimal.** — *1 mark*

6. **Convert the binary value 01101100 to hexadecimal.** — *1 mark*

Representing negative integers in binary

There are two ways to represent negative integers in binary, these are sign and magnitude and two's complement. For sign and magnitude, this is simply using a bit to signify if the number is positive or negative. The bit is placed at the start of the binary number. The name given to this bit is the most significant bit (MSB). If the number is negative, this bit will be 1. If it is positive, this bit will be 0.

In two's complement the MSB is changed to be a negative number. For example, 128 becomes –128. Therefore, we start with a value of –128 and add to this value to represent our negative number. Two's complement is the method used by most computers to represent negative numbers. Another way we can find the two's complement of a number is by taking its positive binary values, flipping them, then adding 1.

7 **Convert the value 25 to 8-bit binary sign and magnitude.**

....

8 **Convert the value −13 to 8-bit binary sign and magnitude.**

....

9 **Convert the value −101 to two's complement 8-bit binary.**

....

10 **Convert the value 88 to two's complement 8-bit binary.**

....

Adding in binary

To add two binary numbers there are four rules to remember:

$0 + 0 = 0$

$0 + 1 = 1$

$1 + 1 = 10$ (the binary value for 2)

$1 + 1 + 1 = 11$ (the binary value for 3)

Therefore, if we add the values:

```
0 0 1 1 1 0 0 0
0 0 0 1 1 1 1 0 +
   1 1 1
0 1 0 1 0 1 1 0
```

we get the binary value 01010110.

We must carry numbers just like we do in normal addition of numbers. The small numbers underneath are the numbers that have been carried. We can add two's complement binary numbers using the same method. If we end up with an extra carry at the end, this is called an overflow.

11 **Add together the binary values 00011100 and 10000001.**

....

....

12 **Add together the binary values 10010101 and 11001001.**

....

....

Subtracting in binary

To subtract binary numbers, we use the normal rules of subtraction, but with an additional extra rule. When we borrow from the next column, we place a value of 2 as the carry. This is because we have borrowed two lots of that unit. For example, if we borrow from the '8' unit column, we place 2 in the '4' unit column as we have borrowed two lots of 4, hence 8. If we cannot borrow from the next column, we have to go to the column after and borrow from that first.

For example:

```
        2 2 1
       ⌀ ⌀⌀ 2
  0 0 ✗ ✗ ✗ ⌀ ⌀ 0 –
  0 0 0 1 1 1 1 0
  ─────────────────
  0 0 0 1 1 0 1 0
```

13 **Subtract the two binary values 11001100 and 01010101.** `2 marks`

....

....

Subtracting using two's complement numbers

To subtract using two's complement there are several stages that we need to go through. For example, let's take the calculation 48 – 22:

We convert the first value to binary: 48 as binary is 00110000.

We convert the second value to the two's complement binary: 22 as binary is 00010110. The two's complement of this is 11101010.

We then add the two values:

```
  0 0 1 1 0 0 0 0
  1 1 1 0 1 0 1 0 +
  ──────────────────
  1 1 1
  0 0 0 1 1 0 1 0
```

We discard the last carry, so we are left with the value 00011010, which is the correct denary value of 26.

14 **Subtract the two binary values 11001100 and 01010101 using two's complement.** `3 marks`

....

....

....

Representing real numbers in binary

So far, we have only been looking at representing integer values in binary. We also need to know how to represent real values in binary. Real numbers in binary have two parts to them, the mantissa and the exponent. The mantissa is a value that will have a floating point and the exponent is the number of places the floating point has 'floated' to the left. The floating point is placed just after the MSB.

For example: 111101111 110 has a mantissa of 1.11101111 and an exponent of 110.

This means that the floating point has been moved six places to the left.

If we move the floating point back six places to the right, we have 1111011.11.

If we convert the values to the left of the floating point, we get 123.

The values after the floating point have fractional values starting with ½. After the floating point there are the values ½ and ¼. These values are added together to make ¾ or .75.

This means that the real number represented by the mantissa and exponent is 123.75.

We can also normalise real values to make sure that we are able to store the largest value possible with the bit allocation that we have.

Show how the value 101.25 is represented as a floating point number with a 6-bit exponent and a 10-bit mantissa.

....

....

....

Convert the following floating point number to its denary value.
- **0.100110111 000111**
- **It has a 10-bit mantissa and a 6-bit exponent.**

....

....

Bitwise manipulation of binary values

We also need to know how to perform bitwise manipulation and use masks on binary values.

In bitwise manipulation, binary values are shifted to the left or to the right. Any empty spaces after the shift are filled with zeros.

Each bit shift to the left is like multiplying the number by two. Each bit shift to the right is like dividing the number by 2.

We can also use masks with our binary values to perform logical operations.

If we take the binary value 10101010 and the mask 11001100, each operation would give us:

AND

1	0	1	0	1	0	1	0
1	1	0	0	1	1	0	0
1	0	0	0	1	0	0	0

OR

1	0	1	0	1	0	1	0
1	1	0	0	1	1	0	0
1	1	1	0	1	1	1	0

XOR

1	0	1	0	1	0	1	0
1	1	0	0	1	1	0	0
0	1	1	0	0	1	1	0

We can use these logical operations to check for different patterns in binary values.

17 Perform a bitwise left shift of three places on the binary value 01100001.

1 mark

18 Perform a bitwise right shift of four places on the binary value 11111101.

1 mark

19 Perform an AND logical operation on the binary value 11011001 with the mask 00010111.

1 mark

Representing text

As all data needs to be converted to binary to be processed by the computer, text also needs to be converted. Text is converted to binary using a character set. Two common character sets are ASCII and UNICODE. In a character set, each letter has an equivalent binary value, for example the binary value for the capital letter A in the ASCII character set is 01000001.

Data structures

Arrays

A one-dimensional array allows us to store one type of data, e.g. a set of test scores. For example:

12	27	56	64	27	43	12	15	45	69

Arrays normally start at an index of 0, so index[3] stored number 64.

A two-dimensional array allows us to store two different types of data, e.g. student's name and three test scores. For example:

Benny	11	13	47
Billy	13	17	33
Boris	45	33	55
Jane	9	32	44
Joanne	54	55	39
Jenna	9	48	31

A two-dimensional array is indexed on both the x and y co-ordinates. Index[0,4] stores Joanne and [2,2] stores 33.

A three-dimensional array allows us to store three different type of data, e.g. student's name, three test scores and two resit scores for each test. Imagine the table above as a three-dimensional shape with two entries behind each test score for the resit values.

20 Define an array in pseudocode that would store 10 students' names and six test scores for each student.

1 mark

21 Define an array in pseudocode that would store 30 students' names, five test scores and three resit scores for each test.

1 mark

Records, lists and tuples

Lists are like a one-dimensional array, but with some differences. Lists are a dynamic structure, they are mutable and slower to access.

Records and tuples are practically the same thing. The main difference is that in tuples just the value is stored; in records, a variable name for each value is stored also. They are a collection of data that is grouped together. Once they are created they are immutable. You could imagine them as being like a row in a database.

22 **Give two differences between a list and an array.**

....

....

23 **State two characteristics of a tuple.**

....

....

....

Stacks and queues

Data can be stored in several different structures. Two structures that can be used are stacks and queues.

A stack can be described as a Last In First Out (LIFO) structure. Data is added to the top of the stack and removed from the top of the stack.

A queue can be described as a First In First Out (FIFO) structure. Data is added to the end of the queue but removed from the front of the queue. Queues can be circular structures.

24 **The following data is stored in a stack: 25, 36, 75, 33, 29, 40.**

The value 25 is the bottom of the stack. Show what the stack would look like after the following operations have been carried out.

POP

PUSH 27

PUSH 13

POP

....

25 **The following data is stored in a circular queue: 25, 36, 75, 33, 29, 40.**

The value 33 is the start of the queue and the value 75 is the end of the queue. Show what the queue would look like after the following operations have been carried out.

POP

PUSH 23

POP

PUSH 99

Make sure you show where the queue would start and end.

....

....

Linked lists, graphs, binary trees and hash tables

A linked list is an ordered set of data, each of which contains a pointer to the next item of data (and sometimes the preceding item of data). Linked lists have two advantages over an array in that they are dynamic and it is easier to add and remove data. Data is added to a linked list using the free space pointer. The pointer from the preceding data item will need to be updated to point to the newly added item. To remove an item from a linked list, the pointer from the preceding item to the one being removed, is changed to point to the new next item of data. A traverse of a linked list will start at the beginning and look at each item in turn until the item required is found.

A graph is a collection of data nodes and the connections between them. There are two approaches to traversing a graph and these are depth-first and breadth-first.

A binary tree is made up of parent and child nodes. A parent node can have two child nodes, a left and a right child.

Hash tables are used to allow direct access to records than are stored in an array. An address of a record in the array is calculated from the key value of a record. This process is called hashing.

26 **State what is meant by a pointer in a linked list.**   1 mark

....

....

27 **The following data is stored as a linked list:**

Option A, Option B, Option C, Option D

Option B will no longer be available, so it needs to be removed from the list.

Explain how option B is removed from the linked list.   3 marks

....

....

....

28 **Explain the difference between traversing a graph using depth-first and breadth-first traversal.**   4 marks

....

....

....

....

....

Boolean algebra
Karnaugh maps

Boolean algebra is a complex topic. You need to be able to simplify Boolean expressions using a Karnaugh map. In order to simplify a Boolean expression using a Karnaugh map the expression needs to be in sum-of-products form. There are several rules that need to be applied when creating a Karnaugh map. Groups:

- can only be created in multiples of 2
- cannot contain cells with 0/blank
- cannot be diagonal

- should be as large as possible
- can overlap
- can 'wrap around' the map

There are several stages that you can follow to create a Karnaugh map:

- Set out the variables for the map.
- Map each term in the Boolean expression with a 1 (or a dot).
- Group the 1s (or dots).
- Identify the constants.

 **Simplify the following Boolean expression using a Karnaugh map.**

$$\neg A \wedge B \wedge C \vee A \wedge \neg B \wedge C \vee A \wedge B \wedge C \wedge \neg \quad A \wedge B \wedge \neg C$$

Simplification rules

Boolean expressions can also be simplified using the rules of simplification. The first rules that you need to understand are often referred to as the rules of double negation, or identity.

$A \wedge A = A$

$A \vee A = A$

$\neg (\neg A) = A$

$A \wedge \neg A = 0$ (False)

$A \vee \neg A = 1$ (True)

Law	AND	OR
Commutative	$A \wedge B = B \wedge A$	$A \vee B = B \vee A$
Associate	$(A \wedge B) \wedge C = A \wedge (B \wedge C)$	$(A \vee B) \vee C = A \vee (B \vee C)$
Distributive	$A \wedge (B \vee C) = A \wedge B \vee A \wedge C$	$A \vee (B \wedge C) = A \vee B \wedge A \vee C$

Table 4 Further rules of simplification

You need to be able to apply these rules to simplify a Boolean expression.

There is a final set of rules that you need to be able to apply. These are called De Morgan's rules. The rules of De Morgan's are:

$\neg (A \vee B) = \neg A \wedge \neg B$

$\neg (A \wedge B) = \neg A \vee \neg B$

Using the laws of simplification, simplify the following Boolean expression.

A ∧ B ∨ B ∧ C ∧ (B ∨ C)

....

....

Logic gates

Logic gates are the foundation of logic processes in a computer. You need to understand the logic of several logic gates, including how to create truth tables for them. The logic gates that you need to understand are AND, OR, NOT, NAND, NOR and XOR. You need to be able to combine these logic gates to create a logic diagram.

Adder circuits

You also need to understand the logic of half and full adders and flip flops.

A fundamental operation in computers is the addition of binary values. A simple circuit that can be used for binary addition is a half adder.

The half adder circuit takes in two inputs and outputs a sum bit and a carry bit.

The logic of a half adder can be shown in a truth table as:

A	B	Sum	Carry
0	0	0	0
0	1	1	0
1	0	1	0
1	1	0	1

A full adder circuit has three inputs, including the previous carry bit.

The logic of a full adder can be shown in a truth table as:

A	B	Carry in	Sum	Carry out
0	0	0	0	0
0	0	1	1	0
0	1	0	1	0
0	1	1	0	1
1	0	0	1	0
1	0	1	0	1
1	1	0	0	1
1	1	1	1	1

Flip-flop circuits

A flip-flop circuit is one of the most fundamental logic circuits in digital technology. A simple flip-flop circuit would be:

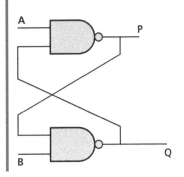

The logic of a flip-flop circuit can be shown in a truth table as:

A	B	P	Q
0	0	1	1
0	1	1	0
1	0	0	1
1	1	0	1
		1	0

Exam-style questions

31 Add the binary floating point values 0100110100 000111 and 0001110110 000110. `4 marks`

32 Perform an XOR logical operation on the binary value 01110001 with the mask 00010111. `1 mark`

33 Explain how the operation of a stack is different to the operation of a queue. `3 marks`

....

....

....

34 Show how the following data would be represented as a binary search tree. `4 marks`

ELM, APPLE, OAK, BEECH, BIRCH, FIR, MAPLE, ASH, PINE, BAY

Write your answer on a separate sheet of paper.

35 Simplify the following Boolean expression using a Karnaugh map. `3 marks`

$B \wedge C \wedge \neg A \vee B \wedge \neg C \wedge A \vee A \wedge \neg B \wedge \neg C \vee \neg B \wedge C \wedge \neg A \vee A \wedge \neg B \wedge C$

Write your answer on a separate sheet of paper.

36 Using the laws of simplification, simplify the following Boolean expression. `4 marks`

$B \wedge \neg B \wedge (A \wedge B) \vee (A \wedge C)$

....

....

....

....

....

....

....

....

Computer law and ethical, moral and social issues

Computer law

There are four main legislative Acts that you need to understand:

- Data Protection Act (1998)
- Computer Misuse Act (1990)
- Copyright Design and Patents Act (1988)
- Regulation of Investigatory Powers Act (2000)

Each Act regulates a different element of the use of data or technology. Computer crime is an increasing issue and governments and legislation are struggling to keep up with advancements in computer crime. A relatively new law that also regulates the use of data is the General Data Protection Regulation (GDPR). This is an EU law that regulates the processing of personal data within the EU. It was designed to make the regulations much clearer for both people and businesses.

1 **Give two principles of the Data Protection Act (1998).**   2 marks

....

....

2 **Explain the purpose of the Regulation of Investigatory Powers Act (2000).**   2 marks

....

....

Ethical, moral and social issues

The development of technology and how we use it has brought about several moral and ethical issues. The introduction of computers into society has created issues in various areas of society. The introduction of computers in the workplace has brought about a fear of job loss and also unease about computers performing certain tasks. The use of computers for automated decision making can also create unease due to the reliance only on logic.

One of the more recent developments at the forefront of moral and ethical issues is the development of artificial intelligence. There is increasing concern expressed that allowing computers to develop something close to a conscience can be a large risk to manage.

Another pressing concern is the effect of computers on the environment. Computers can be made from some toxic materials that need to be handled with great care. If these materials are not disposed of correctly, they can seep into our soil and affect our food systems.

There has been a lot of debate about the accessibility of material using the internet. Some people believe that there should be much more censorship in place, while others think that is a violation of human rights. Some countries have far greater levels of censorship than others. Computers are increasingly used to monitor our behaviour. Again, some people think this is a necessity to keep society safe, but others believe it creates a nanny state and is a violation of human rights.

Computers are used to mine vast amounts of data that is analysed by organisations. The analysing of our information in this way is also seen as controversial. People worry about the amount of data that organisations hold about us and the danger and security issues that surround this.

An increasing problem with technology is the issue of piracy. Some people believe the entertainment industry charges too much for the products they create. This has led to some people pirating copies of the product.

3 State two benefits and one drawback to the workers of introducing computers into the workplace.

....

....

....

4 Explain what is meant by artificial intelligence and why some people believe it is a risk.

....

....

....

....

....

5 Explain two environmental concerns arising from using computers.

....

....

....

....

Exam-style questions

25

6 Discuss the implications of the Data Protection Act on a company gathering data for marketing and selling it to global organisations.　9 marks

....

....

....

....

....

....

....

....

....

....

....

....

....

7 Consider the following statement:

Some people believe that there is too much censorship of content available on the internet, believing this to be a violation of human rights. Others believe that there is not enough censorship and more should be put in place.

Discuss the merits of this statement.

11 marks

Cover photo: AndSus/Fotolia

Hachette UK's policy is to use papers that are natural, renewable and recyclable products and made from wood grown in well-managed forests and other controlled sources. The logging and manufacturing processes are expected to conform to the environmental regulations of the country of origin.

Orders: please contact Hachette UK Distribution, Hely Hutchinson Centre, Milton Road, Didcot, Oxfordshire, OX11 7HH.
Telephone: (44) 01235 827827.
E-mail education@hachette.co.uk Lines are open from 9 a.m. to 5 p.m., Monday to Friday. You can also order through our website: www.hoddereducation.co.uk

ISBN: 978-1-5104-3699-2

© Sarah Lawrey 2019

First published in 2019 by

Hodder Education,
an Hachette Company,
Carmelite House,
50 Victoria Embankment,
London, EC4Y 0DZ

www.hoddereducation.co.uk

Impression number   10 9 8

Year   2024

Typeset by Aptara, India

Printed in the UK

A catalogue record for this title is available from the British Library.

HODDER EDUCATION
t: 01235 827827
e: education@hachette.co.uk
w: hoddereducation.co.uk

ISBN 978-1-5104-3699-2

MIX
Paper | Supporting responsible forestry
FSC™ C104740